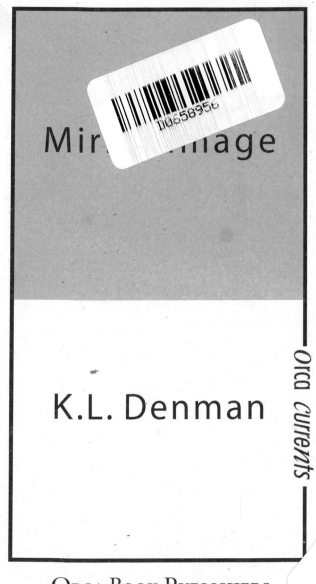

Mirror Image

K.L. Denman

Orca *Currents*

ORCA BOOK PUBLISHERS

Library and Archives Canada Cataloguing in Publication

Denman, K. L., 1957-
Mirror image / written by K.L. Denman.

(Orca currents)
ISBN 978-1-55143-667-8 (bound)
ISBN 978-1-55143-665-4 (pbk.)

I. Title. II. Series.

PS8607.E64M57 2007   jC813'.6   C2006-906392-3

Summary: Inspired by a school art project and a new friend,
Sable learns to look beneath the surface of an image.

First published in the United States, 2007
Library of Congress Control Number: 2006938224

Orca Book Publishers gratefully acknowledges the support for its publishing
programs provided by the following agencies: the Government of Canada
through the Book Publishing Industry Development Program and the
Canada Council for the Arts, and the Province of British Columbia
through the BC Arts Council and the Book Publishing Tax Credit.

Cover design: Doug McCaffry
Cover photography: Jupiterimages

Orca Book Publishers
PO Box 5626, Station B
Victoria, BC Canada
V8R 6S4

Orca Book Publishers
PO Box 468
Custer, WA USA
98240-0468

www.orcabook.com
Printed and bound in Canada.
Printed on 100% PCW recycled paper.

10 09 08 07 • 4 3 2 1

For Hannah—May you find true beauty, always.
KLD

I'm ever grateful to Diane Tullson and Shelley Hrdlitschka for their wisdom. My thanks also to Tiffany Stark for her enthusiastic support, to Jasmine Kovac for sharing her Bosnian heritage, and to Melanie Jeffs, Orca Currents Editor, for her insightful questions.

There are two ways of spreading light: to be the candle or the mirror that reflects it.

—Edith Wharton

chapter one

I feel that doom is near. This feeling makes me angry and nervous. I keep looking for the cause and can't find it. It could be that aliens are finally going to attack and turn us into slaves. Or we're all going to catch the flu and puke to death. Or the holes in the ozone layer will grow so big we'll be fried by the sun. Or maybe the senior humans will do something really stupid, like start the third world war and kaboom. Game over.

How's a girl supposed to cope with this? I hate the big cloud of dread that hangs over me. I want to get rid of it, take control. So what do people do when they can't stand the way things are?

I've made lists:

- Become a politician (I doubt anyone would vote for me.)
- Join a secret underground group (How do you find secret underground groups?)
- Become a scientist and invent alien detectors. Or ozone menders. Or an auto-kill switch for nuclear weapons. (No way would I wear a white lab coat. I wear only black.)

I decided to wear only black when I was thirteen and my mother bought me a frilly lime green dress. Who wants to be caught wearing lime green on the day the world ends?

There's this girl in my art class who would die wearing hot pink if our doom arrived today. She always wears pink. Of all the people on the planet, she annoys me more than anyone else. Her name is Lacey and she's quite the experiment in Artificial Stupidity. For example, I heard her telling one of the other girls about her boyfriend.

"Chad is so, like, perfect for me, right? Because he's just soooo cute! He has an amazing six-pack and white teeth and such good hair. And he knows how to dress! I mean, when I'm with him, it's like having the best purse or something, right? We just look so good together!"

She actually thinks her boyfriend is some sort of fashion accessory.

I've never talked to Lacey because, clearly, it would be a waste of breath. I don't even know why people like her were born. What is she good for? Proof that evolution can go backward? Sure, she's pretty, but that's about it. Dolls are pretty too, and I got bored with them years ago. Meh. I hardly ever played with them even when I was little. Why would I bother with a brainless doll now?

Sadly these things can be forced on us.

chapter two

I don't especially like art, but I'm taking it anyway. My school says all grade nine students must take something artsy, and it was art, music or drama. Not exactly fair when I suck at all of them and would rather be in science. But here again, I have no power to change things. So I'm in art class and the teacher, Mr. Ripley, asks us to give him suggestions for our final project. He's a good one, the sort of teacher who is honestly interested in what kids have to say.

I do not raise my hand. But Lacey does.

"Yes, Lacey?" he says.

"This is the coolest idea, Mr. Ripley! I read about it in the paper. Okay, I didn't read the paper, but my dad did, and he, like, told me about it. Some artists on Vancouver Island are making these old school mirrors, right? People used to make these mirrors, like, a few hundred years ago and now these artists are making them again."

"Why is that?" Mr. Ripley asks.

"Okay. So. First of all, they make the frames really fancy, right? The original frames were carved out of wood. Now they're using wood pulp to form them."

"Wood pulp?"

"Yeah," she says. Then she giggles and adds, "Believe it or not."

I can't believe she said that. So lame. Mr. Ripley must have heard it about a thousand times by now. A few idiots in the class actually laugh at Lacey's joke. She tosses her long blond hair and keeps yapping.

"But I bet we could make the frame out of papier-mâché."

Mr. Ripley's expression hasn't changed. He still looks interested in what Lacey is saying. He strokes his chin and says, "Papier-mâché sounds like a good substitute. So you want to make a unique mirror frame?"

"Right!" Lacey is bouncing in her seat now, looking very excited. "But that's not all. The really cool thing about the mirrors is that a piece of poetry goes on the back."

Mr. Ripley's brows slant down. "I'm sorry. I don't quite see the purpose of that. Why would you put poetry behind the mirror? No one would be able to see it."

Some of the more intelligent life forms in the class are shaking their heads and rolling their eyes.

Lacey doesn't notice. Her face is glowing as she goes on. "Right! But that's the whole point. See, the person who owns the mirror knows the poem is there. They know what it says, even though it gets, like, sealed on the back of the mirror. What happens is, they look at themselves in the mirror and think about the poem, right?"

Mr. Ripley is silent. He taps his long fingers on the desk. Finally he looks at her and smiles, just a little. "Tell me, Lacey. Why does this interest you?"

"Because when you look in that mirror, your reflection is there with the poem behind, right? It would feel as if the poem is, like, *inside* you."

Now his smile is huge. "Or maybe it means there's more to the image than meets the eye. I like this, Lacey. Very much. I'm going to add it to our list. Thank you for the suggestion. Anyone else have an idea they'd like to propose?"

There are more suggestions. Someone wants us to design CD cover art for their friend's band. Someone else wants us to paint a mural on the wall of the principal's office. I don't pay much attention because I'm thinking about what Mr. Ripley said. More to the image than meets the eye. Hah.

I come back to the moment when I hear my name being called. "Sable? Your vote?"

I look around. Most of the class has their hands in the air. I put mine up too.

"All right then," says Mr. Riply. "It looks like our final project will be the mirror."

I voted for Lacey's mirror? It figures.

chapter three

Mom is excited. This is not always a good thing. As I walk into the kitchen I hear her voice rising and falling, the Bosnian words flowing fast. She's talking on the phone. She waves at me and then turns away and keeps talking. This is one of those little ironies about her. She's upset that I don't speak Bosnian as well as I should, yet when she wants to talk about something she doesn't want me to hear, she forgets English real quick.

She hasn't figured out that although I don't speak the language very well, I understand quite a lot. Like now, she's talking about Dad. I listen more closely. Her voice drops to a whisper. Then she laughs like a maniac. Says she'll call back later. *Ciao.*

She turns to me with a huge smile, eyes dancing. "Sable! How was your day?"

I give my usual answer. "Fine."

"Good. You can help make dinner. Wash vegetables." She sticks her head into the fridge and starts hauling stuff out.

"Who was on the phone?" I ask.

She looks at me narrowly. "Why?"

I shrug. "Just wondering. It sounded like you were laughing at Dad."

She flings her arm up like a kid in class with all the right answers—her favorite European gesture—and says, "*Phht*! It's nothing. Women jokes."

"Whatever," I say. And I start walking.

"Sable! Vegetables. And what is this *whatever* you are always saying?"

I fling my arm up and say, "*Phht*! It's nothing."

"What about vegetables?"

I roll my eyes. "Why don't you ask the twins to help you? They're old enough."

Mom folds her arms across her chest. "Boys are at soccer practice. And I asked you."

"I have a lot of homework," I lie.

Her expression softens. "Oh. You do homework then. Get good grades, is so important. You are so smart."

Now I feel guilty. I sigh and say, "Thanks, Mom." And I make my escape.

I don't really have much homework. I'm supposed to start thinking about a quote for my mirror. Oh, and gather newspaper to bring to class for making papier-mâché. Not exactly a lot of work. I should help make dinner.

But I don't. I sit in my room and wonder if my mom could be having an affair. After all, Dad isn't her first love. Her first love was my father who I don't even remember. He was killed when we were trying to escape the war in Bosnia. Mom and I made it out, and then we came to Canada. She said she didn't especially want to come here, but we had to go somewhere. The United States and some other countries were taking refugees too, and she just told the person sorting us out to pick a country for her. She didn't care. I was only three years old and I didn't care either.

She says it worked out for the best. She loves Canada. She told me she used to think she should have asked to be sent to New York with her sister. But then she wouldn't have met my new dad, and she says that would have been awful. They met about a year after we got here; they got married and he adopted me. A couple years later, she had the twins, my half-brothers, Todd and Tyler. For snotty little brothers, they're okay. And Dad's really nice. Mom thinks everything is great.

So I wonder what quote describes me best? I look into the mirror and see me. Same old straight black hair. Same old brown eyes. New zit on the chin. I don't see any poetry.

chapter four

Art class is crazy. Some of the kids are
wadding up newspaper and throwing it
around the room. Others are using the
papier-mâché glop to paint their faces. They
wait for it to dry, then peel it off, shrieking
about how gross it looks. Is this grade six
or grade nine? No one could tell by looking.
There are a few kids discussing the quotes
they've chosen for their mirror. I suppose
this could be considered mature?

There's a girl saying, "That was my idea. I said it first."

The other girl replies, "So what? You think you own it? Get lost."

Girl number one: "You get lost!"

Girl number two: "Now look who's copying! You get lost!"

No. This is definitely not mature.

I catch another conversation. A guy is telling Lacey, "I've got my quote. I'm gonna use that line from the U2 song. *I still haven't found what I'm looking for.*"

I think that's pretty funny. Clever.

Lacey frowns. "What do you mean by that, Rav? Didn't you just say you, like, know what your quote will be?"

Is she slow, or what?

Rav raises his eyebrows and stares at her for a second.

I can't help myself. I speak without thinking. "Duh, Lacey. If he puts that line behind the mirror, he's saying he's still searching for himself. Or...," I hesitate before adding, "he's saying that he isn't happy with what he sees."

Rav stares at me now. He looks like he just noticed my existence. Like maybe I was invisible until this moment. He says, "Yeah. Yeah, um, what's your name again?"

"Sable."

"Right. Sable. You got it."

Lacey tosses her blond hair. "Okay, I get it too, Rav. But isn't that, like, negative?"

Rav shrugs. "Maybe. But it's the truth."

I don't say anything else because a wayward wad of newspaper nails me right between the eyes. Mr. Ripley chooses that moment to return to class. The girls arguing about their quote don't notice him right away and one of them screeches, "You're such a stupid cow."

Mr. Ripley is not impressed. He roars, "That's enough!"

Everyone freezes. I don't think any of us knew he had that kind of volume. We wait, some of us watching him, some of us looking at the tabletops. I figure we're in for a class detention and I hate that. I don't know how many times I've sat in detention after school because my classmates are morons.

He takes his time. He looks around at each one of us and makes eye contact. For those who are staring at the tabletop, he waits. They can feel his gaze and sooner or later, they all look up. I've never seen Mr. Ripley so angry.

At last, he speaks. "What is art?" he asks.

This must be a trick question. Nobody answers.

"Never thought about it before?" He pauses, rubs his jaw. "There are many definitions of art." He touches the rose in the vase on his desk. "Some say it's intended to create beauty."

He taps his forehead. "Some say it's meant to communicate a thought or an idea that is best shared visually."

Mr. Ripley strolls across the room, takes an art history book off a shelf and flips through the pages. "Some say it makes a record of time and place, or that it's a measure of culture."

He puts the book down and opens his arms wide. "Others say art is none of these things; it simply exists for its own sake."

He makes his way back to his desk, leans against it and looks at us. "I will not tell you what art is. That's for you to decide. With this final project, I hoped that each of you would find a way to understand art at a personal level. However..."

Long pause.

"However, I do not see you taking this opportunity for introspection. Do you know what that means? It means looking inside yourself. I hoped each of you would look inside and try to find a bit of yourself to put into a piece of art."

Wow. Who knew he expected that from us? Even I missed it.

He starts rubbing his jaw again. Then he smiles. This is not the normal Mr. Ripley smile. I'd say the smile is tinged with evil. He claps his hands together and says, "Here's what we're going to do. I'm going to assign partners. You will spend time with this partner and try to get to know something vital about that person."

I have a very bad feeling about this.

He goes on. "Then, you will find a quote that you believe describes your partner. You will present your partner with this quote, and you will explain why you chose it."

My mouth is dry. Lacey's mirror has morphed into a nightmare.

He's not done yet. "Your partner does *not* have to use the quote you provide, but he or she will benefit from your input."

One of the "get lost" girls puts her hand up.

"Yes?" Mr. Ripley says.

"Can we choose our partner?"

"Oh no," he replies. And that evil smile is back. "I will select the partners. And be prepared. I've had the entire term to observe this class. I know who hangs out with whom. None of you will be partnered with a friend. I will announce the list tomorrow."

A moan escapes from nearly everybody in the room. Not from me. I feel too ill to moan. A class detention is looking real good right now.

chapter five

There's quite the reaction when Mr. Ripley reads out the partners. Some people smirk. Others swear under their breath. One girl actually bursts into tears.

My partner is Lacey. I should have known. Really, I should have. Cruel doom. She looks at me with startled blue eyes. Her mouth forms a small circle. Then she says, "Wow. Too random."

What is that supposed to mean? It turns out that I've said this out loud.

Lacey giggles and says, "Nothing. Really. So I guess we're going to have to get together and, like, chill, huh?"

I say, "Yeah, *like*, I guess so."

She blinks a few times. She actually noticed me mocking her use of *like*? Maybe not, because she's smiling again when she says, "Okay. We'll go to your house after school."

What? She thinks I'm going to take her home with me? I figure I could learn all I need to know about her in less than ten minutes. I shake my head and say, "I don't think so."

Of course Mr. Ripley chooses that moment to get even nastier. "If possible, try to visit one another at home. People are often more comfortable in familiar places. It might make it easier for you to get to know your partner."

Before Lacey can take control again, I say, "Let's go to your place first."

Lacey frowns. Then she shrugs, looks away and mutters, "Whatever."

I feel like I've scored. I don't know why, but it's like I just won some sort of a point.

"Cool. I'll meet you by the flagpole after school?"

"Sure, see you then." And she turns her back on me. Sore loser.

Lacey doesn't show up at the flagpole. I wait for twenty minutes, and then I go home. I'm in a very bad mood when I get there and when Mom asks, "How was your day?" I don't bother to reply. I just walk right past her and go straight to my room.

Big mistake. One minute later, she's knocking on my door. "Sable? What is wrong? Can I come in?"

"Nothing is wrong. I just need to be alone. Go away."

Her voice rises. "Sable! You should talk to me. Maybe have snack."

I don't answer.

She opens the door and peeks in.

I snarl, "What are you doing?"

"I think maybe you spend too much time alone. Is not so good."

"What do you know?" I sneer. "This is normal for kids in Canada."

Her eyes go wide and sad, and then her mouth crumples into a wobbly line. "Is it?" she whispers.

I feel like crap. Why does she have to do this to me, make me feel guilty? It's like there's some sort of thread between us, a line that ties us together. Every time I'm upset, her mom radar goes off and she starts harassing me. I think that thread needs to be broken.

"Yes," I say, "this is normal."

"But," she says. Then she stops and shakes her head. "But, Sable, I miss you."

"No, Mom," I answer. I force myself to look at her steadily. "I just remind you of my father. You miss him. You miss Bosnia."

She recoils as if I'd hit her. "No! That is not so! I am happy here, very happy. Safe."

"Safe?" I ask. "Are you sure?"

"Yes," she insists, "I am sure. There are no soldiers. No bombs. We are safe."

I can think of several things I'd like to say. She's wrong; there are soldiers and bombs and guns here. We just don't see them too often. Plus, she sidestepped my point about her missing Bosnia. I know she does. She talks about going "home" to visit one day. Another thing I could ask is if she's only happy because she feels safe. How lame is that?

But all the anger suddenly leaves me. I just say, "Whatever, Mom."

She stands there for about ten seconds, staring at me, and then she goes without another word.

About two minutes later, she's back, handing me the phone. "A girl calling you," she says. I take the phone and Mom stands there watching me. I turn away from her and mutter, "Hello?"

"Hey, Sable. It's Lacey. How come you, like, ditched me after school?"

She's unbelievable. "I didn't. I waited at the flagpole for twenty minutes."

"The flagpole? Really?" Then she giggles. "Oh right! You *did* say that. Silly me. I was waiting by the gym door."

I don't say anything.

Lacey bubbles on. "So, like, I guess you're at home now."

I have to ask, "What was your first clue?"

Giggle. Giggle more. "Well, I'm sorry. So if you want, I can just come over to your place."

"No," I say, "you can't come to my place."

And there's my mother, yelling like a soccer fan, "Yes! It's fine. She can come over."

"Um," says Lacey, "so, should I come over, or not?"

Mom is waving her arms. "Is not a problem. Your friend can come, Sable."

I cover up the receiver and hiss at her, "Would you shut up?"

Mom's face gets red. "Shame on you, Sable, speaking to your mother like that!"

She has no idea what other things I'd like to say. None of them are nice. And there's Lacey's voice again, "Hello? Hello?"

"Fine!" I shout into the receiver. "Come over."

"Cool. I got your address from the

phone book, but can you tell me what color your house is? I'm not so great with numbers."

"It's green, okay? With white trim. And there's a blue van in the driveway. Is that enough information for you?"

"That's awesome," she coos. "Be there soon. Bye."

I don't say good-bye. I just hang up.

chapter six

Mom gets over her anger quickly when she hears that Lacey is coming over. "Wonderful! Shall I make snack for you?"

"Mom," I say, "no. Lacey is not my friend. She's just someone I got stuck doing homework with, okay? I don't like her. She's a freak."

Mom frowns. "Freak? What is wrong? You mean she is disabled? Doesn't matter. You should be kind to this freak person."

I don't have the strength to explain. I nod wearily. "Fine, Mom. Whatever."

"Whatever," she repeats. "I think I am knowing what this means now." She does her arm fling and says, "*Phht*!"

When the doorbell rings, I don't rush to answer it. I slowly make my way to the door, but Mom beats me to it. She whips the door open, smiles and holds out her hand. "Welcome! Come in."

I can see Lacey standing on the step, blinking. She nervously eyeballs Mom's outstretched hand. In a gentle voice, Mom encourages Lacey. "It's all right. Please, come in."

Great. Obviously Mom assumes Lacey has a mental disability. Which when you think about it, is true. Mom gives up on the handshake. Instead she starts waving her arm in a circle like one of those traffic people on the side of the road.

Lacey takes a small step and says, "Um. Hi. Is Sable here?"

"Yes, yes. Come in." Mom opens the door wider and keeps up the traffic routine.

Lacey catches sight of me waiting outside the range of Mom's arm and smiles with relief.

"Hey," she says, "I wasn't sure I had the right place."

"This is it," I say. Now what? I don't especially want Lacey in my room, but Mom is still hovering, hands fluttering, and it would be best to avoid her. If we stay downstairs, she's likely to bring out milk and cookies.

"Come on." I gesture for Lacey to follow. Once we're in my room, she prowls around, looking at everything. Nosey. She checks out my black bedspread, the black and white photos, the glossy black desk, the black vase holding fake black roses.

"So," she says, "I'm guessing your favorite color is black?"

I drop my gaze to her vivid pink sneakers. "And yours is pink?"

She ignores my question. "Is black really a color?" She doesn't wait for me to answer. "I don't think it is. It's, like, a non-color, isn't it?"

"Sort of," I say. "It absorbs all the light."

"Wow. Don't you think that's, like, depressing?"

"What would someone like *you* know about it?" I ask.

She stares at me. I've never seen that particular expression on her face before. It makes her look different, like someone else. Someone with a brain. "Sable," she says, "this art project is important to me. I need to get a good mark. Can we just work on the assignment?"

I shrug. "What do you mean?"

"Well, I'm here to get to know you, aren't I? Whether you like it or not. So why don't you just give the whole hostility thing a rest?"

I shake my head. "Maybe we ought to ask Mr. Ripley for different partners."

She does an eye roll and admits, "I already tried. That's where I was after school. I told him that we're, like, opposites, and chances are we couldn't understand each other."

It takes a second or two for this to sink in. She lied? And she tried to get rid of me? Not exactly surprising, but why is she admitting it?

"I'm sorry, okay?" she blurts. "But I figured you felt the same. You don't like me one bit, do you?"

"So?" I ask coldly. "What did he say?"

"He said that's exactly why he put us together. We're supposed to get past our differences. And so then I thought, okay, I can do that. I mean, why not?"

"Why did you lie to me?"

Lacey frowns. "Why don't you answer my question?"

"What question?"

"The one about you not liking me. I mean, come on. It's so obvious. And since you wanted a different partner too, what's your problem with me asking Mr. Ripley?"

"You shouldn't have lied," I say.

"Okay! I said I'm sorry. Look, can we just do this? Mr. Ripley said no matter how great our frames turn out, our final mark depends on what he called 'meaningful discovery.'"

"You've got to be kidding."

"I'm not. That's what he said. Sucks, huh?"

I sink down onto my bed. "Yeah."

Lacey slumps down beside me. For some reason, this doesn't bother me the way it should. Maybe it's because we have something in common now. We're both victims of Mr. Ripley's cruelty.

"So," says Lacey, "I guess we have to deal with it."

She's probably right, but I consider my options. I could fake a major illness and miss the next couple weeks of school. Only then I'd get crappy marks in everything. Plus I'd probably have to take art over again next year. Run away? Nah, too extreme. I can't think of any other options.

"Forget it," I say. "It's not worth it."

Lacey sits up straight. "You mean you're not going to do it?"

"No," I say, "I mean I *am* going to do it."

She looks at me with the same nervous face she had when she met Mom: eyes wide and watchful. Slowly, she says, "Ohhh-kaaay. Now that we've got that settled, should we start over?"

This girl can actually focus when she wants to. She doesn't even wait for me to answer. She keeps going. "So, have you thought about what color your mirror frame will be?"

My turn to do an eye roll. "Can't you guess?"

She grins. "Black?"

I can't help it. I grin back. "You got it. And yours will be, uh, pink?"

Her forehead wrinkles. "I don't know yet. I was thinking about maybe, like, a rainbow."

"Oh."

"Yeah. The whole top of the frame will be shaped like a rainbow."

I start picturing this and get an image of the baby room my mom decorated when the twins were born. Ick. "Are you going to make puffy clouds for the bottom part of the frame?" I ask.

She shakes her head. "No. That would be too cute. I was thinking about lightning bolts underneath. I haven't decided for sure yet. What about you?"

I haven't thought about it at all. I do now and, *bam*, I get a great idea. "I'm going to make the frame look like a snake curling around the mirror."

"Eeeuw," says Lacey.

"What?" I ask.

"Well, think about it. You'd look in the mirror and it would be like a snake is wrapped around your face."

She has a point. I feel torn. On the one hand, she's right, a snake around my face *could* be creepy. On the other hand, I don't want to admit I'm wrong. So I defend my idea. "What's wrong with that? Maybe seeing a snake around my face will be a reminder that I need to watch out for enemies. And I'll make it look really cool, black with emerald eyes."

"You need to watch out for enemies?"

I shrug. I'm not about to explain *that* to her.

Lacey frowns. "I don't get you at all. You're not a Goth, right? I mean, hello, you don't wear any makeup. So are you, like, a witch or something?" she asks.

I open my mouth to say no, but then I close it again. And I just smile.

Lacey stands up. "Well, I better go now. So, this was a start anyway. Right?"

"Yeah," I say, "it was. Should we go to your place tomorrow?"

She hesitates, looks around my room, stares at the black roses and gives a little shiver. "Um, yeah. Sure."

chapter seven

The school grounds are practically deserted, and I'm ready to give up on Lacey again when she finally shows at the flagpole. She's twirling a long strand of hair around her finger, round and round. She's also putting a lot of energy into chewing a gigantic wad of bubble gum.

"Hey," she says.

I answer, "Hey."

"So." Chew, chew, twirl. "My place is this way."

She starts walking very fast. Then she slows down. Speeds up. Slows down. I start wondering. She never said a word to me in art class. She hasn't looked directly at me once. Is she embarrassed to be seen with me? Or is she afraid that I'm going to cast a spell on her?

Then she blows a bubble and it explodes into a big blob on her face. She reaches for it with the hair twirling finger. The obvious happens.

"Oh no!" she shrieks.

It's pretty bad, all right. The hair, the finger, the gum, all have bonded. Lacey yanks her finger free and yelps, "Ow!"

"Um," I say, "do you want some help?"

"No! Not unless you know some magic trick to fix it!"

"Oh." I look off into the distance. "About that. I'm not really a witch."

"Well, duh! Only a total idiot would believe you are." She does an eye roll and starts nibbling on the gum mess. When she bites off a piece of gum and spits it out, a tuft of gummy hair goes with it. "Oh my God!" she wails.

"You know," I say, "I didn't think stuff like this happened to girls like you."

Lacey is staring at the nipped hair tuft in horror. It looks like a diseased caterpillar lying on the sidewalk. Without looking up she mumbles, "What?"

"I mean, I thought your life was just naturally perfect."

Now she looks at me. "Are you, like, crazy? You are, aren't you?"

"No," I say hastily, "I'm not. Not really. You should try ice. That's supposed to work."

Lacey takes a step away from me. "Ice? What are you talking about?"

"You put ice on the gum, and then it gets hard and you can scrape it out of your hair."

"Really? Are you sure?"

"No," I admit, "the only certainty is death."

Lacey holds up a hand. "Okay. That's it. Just stop being so freakin' weird for one minute, will you?"

I shrug. "I can try. I'm not promising anything."

"Of course you're not. But Sable, I want you to focus here on what's, like, important. Try to remember." Lacey's voice intensifies. "Will the ice work or won't it?"

I almost laugh, but I sense that would be the wrong thing to do. Possibly even dangerous. I mean, people have been slapped for less. Not that Lacey has ever seemed like that sort, but still. No point in taking chances. "Lacey," I say, "I think the ice works. Either that or peanut butter."

"Great," she says. "Let's go."

She starts walking again, even faster than before. Then she starts twirling the hair again, and I start worrying that she might blow another bubble. I'd rather that whole scene didn't happen again. So I say, "You seem kind of stressed today."

"Wouldn't you be stressed if you, like, totally destroyed your hair?" she asks.

This time I do laugh. It comes out in a snort. "Your hair isn't totally destroyed. What a drama queen!"

Lacey stops. Gives me a look I've been getting from girls since grade six. It's a mix of pity and disgust. I *hate* that look. And then I'm snarling, "What? Do I stink or something?"

She blinks. "Huh?"

"Never mind! I don't know why I'm asking *you*. You're too good to waste your time on me, right? You're so freaked about being with me that you stick gum in your hair."

Lacey shakes her head. "I don't know what you're talking about. This isn't about you at all. It's my place that stinks."

"What?"

"I don't usually bring people home, okay? That's why I'm stressing. But I have to bring you over to get a good mark, don't I?"

I don't know what to say. What could be so bad about her place? And does she mean the only reason she's with me is to get a good mark? Of course that's the only reason she's with me. That's the only reason I'm with her too. Now *I'm* feeling stressed. I shouldn't have reacted to the look. I should have ignored it. I wish I had some gum to chew.

"Well," I mutter, "we probably only have to go to your place once, right? Then we'll be done with this."

"You think? I doubt it, Sable. We didn't get too far yesterday, did we? I mean, you gave me that garbage about being a witch and that was pretty much it. I don't have a clue about a quote for you yet."

She has a point. We walk in silence until she stops abruptly and says, "So, um, this is it."

Lacey has stopped in front of the dumpiest little old house I've ever seen. Green slime is growing up the side. The fence is sagging and the yard is dirt and weeds. A garbage can off to the side has been knocked over and trash is strewn everywhere. Sparkly Lacey lives here?

"Yeah, right," I scoff.

She doesn't say anything. She just marches right up the driveway and goes around the back of the house. I shuffle along behind her and when we get to the back door, I notice the paint is peeling off in large chunks. "You think this is bad," she says, "just wait until you see the inside."

I don't want to see the inside. It's probably filthy, stuff piled everywhere, cobwebs and mold...But I follow Lacey in and don't find what I expected. Quite the opposite. I even feel dizzy for a second because the inside doesn't match the outside at all.

We're standing inside a tiny laundry room, and everything is pure white. The walls, the floor, the appliances. Everything. And it smells like bleach, not mould.

"Don't move until you take your shoes off," Lacey warns. She points to the closet where I see she's already placed her shoes. I slide my black runners in beside Lacey's pink ones and feel guilty over the bit of dirt I see clinging to a shoe lace.

"Come on," Lacey says, "we've got to get some ice."

The kitchen is even more bizarre. White again, but to an impossible extreme. The cupboards, the table and chairs, even the canisters and utensils on the counter are white. The place is so stark and bright, it hurts my eyes. When Lacey opens the freezer, I get my first glimpse of color, a bag of frozen peas. At least their food isn't white.

Lacey is holding a tray of ice cubes and frowning. "Okay, like, now what?"

"Um. Maybe put the ice into a glass, and then stick your hair in there for a while."

Lacey does this, and then she stands awkwardly at the sink, her head tilted to one side. After about ten seconds she says, "This is hurting my neck."

"I don't think you have to stand up," I say. "You could sit down at the table."

Lacey's lower lip juts out in a little pout, but she does what I suggest. She sets the glass down, and then she sits with her head bowed, staring at the gummy clump of hair. "This sucks," she says.

"Yeah," I say.

"No, I mean it really sucks. Like, what happens if my mom catches me?"

"Your mom?" I glance around but don't see anyone.

"She's not here right now. With any luck

she won't show up. But if she finds one speck of gum on her table she'll rant for a week."

I don't think Lacey is kidding. I erupt in a high-pitched giggle.

"It's not funny!" Lacey says.

"Sorry. I guess I'm nervous."

"*You're* nervous? You're not the one who'll have to listen to her. *Your* mom seems really nice."

"She only seems that way," I say defensively. "Believe me, she has tons of weirdness."

"Hah," says Lacey. "Nobody's as weird as my mother. You haven't seen our living room yet."

Now I want to go into the living room. But Lacey is still absorbed with her hair, and I sit down beside her. "Maybe I can help. Let's see if the gum is frozen."

Lacey shoots me a suspicious glance, and then she shrugs. "Okay. But be careful."

I poke a finger into the glass and touch the gum. "It feels cold," I report.

"Good. Now what?"

"Now you can probably pull the gum off your hair."

Lacey lifts her hair out of the glass, grabs the gum wad and yanks. "Ow!" she squeals.

"Not like that," I say. "Let me try." I take hold of the gum and dig in a fingernail. I manage to pick off a fairsized chunk. I flick my finger, and the chip of gum lands on the floor.

"Quick," Lacey says, "pick it up."

I scramble for the offending blob of pink, and I'm down on the floor when a pair of white stiletto heels clatters in. Lacey's mom doesn't take her shoes off, and the heels look dangerous at eye level.

She stares down at me like I'm a big nasty bug and says, "Lacey, what the hell is going on?"

"Nothing," Lacey says.

"Nothing," her mom mimics. "Come off it." She points a long finger at me. "Who's this?"

"This is Sable. My art partner."

Again, Lacey's mom glares at me like I'm

something repulsive. I'm on my feet now, but for half a second, I wonder if I should have stayed on the floor.

Lacey's mom looks like she just stepped out of the pages of a fashion magazine. She's glossy, from the crown of her blond hair, to the shine of her lip-gloss, to the sheen of her blue satin suit and those polished white heels. She's so shiny I wonder if she's coated in a layer of varnish. She also has the coldest hardest pair of blue eyes I've ever seen. Her face has no expression at all; it's frozen, like a painting.

I glance at Lacey and am shocked to see her wearing the exact same face. No emotion, her eyes blank.

"Your art partner?" The cold gaze hits me once more; then it turns to the glass on the table. "Is this your project? What are you doing?"

Lacey tries to hide the glass with her hand. "Nothing."

Shiny Mom grabs the glass, and Lacey's gummy hair swings into view. "Ugh!" says

Shiny Mom. And she shudders. "How incredibly disgusting."

"Yeah," says Lacey.

Shiny Mom reaches into a drawer, whips out a pair of scissors, grabs a hunk of Lacey's hair and snips. It all happens so fast that Lacey reacts in slow motion. Her mouth opens wide. Her eyes open wide. Her hand reaches for her hair. And then she screams. "Ahhhhhhh! My hair! How could you?"

Shiny Mom shudders again as she carries the gummy hair blob to the garbage. "You've *got* to be kidding, Lacey. This is revolting. Now maybe you ought to take your little friend away. I've had a bad day, you know?"

chapter eight

I take Lacey to my house. I don't think Lacey especially wants to come, but I don't think she knows what else to do. She just walks beside me and we don't talk. She doesn't cry either. I keep glancing at her, expecting to see sniffles, but there's nothing. In fact, it's scary, because she looks exactly like her mother.

When we get to my place, my mom is there, like always, cooking something. "Sable! Hello! How was your day? Oh, and you have friend too. Great! Shall I make snack?"

She embarrasses me. She does. Doesn't she know that I'm not a little kid anymore? And right now, even though I should appreciate this when I compare it to what Lacey has, I'm even more embarrassed. I don't understand it, not really, but it's like I have too much mother.

I say, "We're just going to my room, Mom."

I notice Lacey's gaze lingering on a plate of cookies and I say, "But a snack would be good. Can we take some cookies?"

"Yes! Of course! Take them." Mom hands me the whole plate and I turn to go.

Lacey mutters, "Thanks, Mrs....uh, Sable's mom."

Mom does her arm thing and says, "*Phht*! It's nothing. But please, call me Sofija. We are not so fussy here." Then she spots Lacey's hair. It does look bad. Long everywhere except for the big chunk missing on one side. "Oh my goodness! What has happened to you?"

Nice one, Mom. I mean, couldn't she show a little tact? Nope, not her. Whatever thought pops into her head just has to come flying out of her mouth. And then it gets worse. Now Lacey starts to cry.

"Ach!" Mom says, and she hugs Lacey. She pats Lacey's back and says, "There, there. Is not so bad. We can fix."

This last bit scares me. Mom used to cut my hair all the time until I told her she didn't know what she was doing and I needed to go to a real hairdresser. Not that the real hairdresser does any better, but still.

"Mom," I say, "you're not cutting her hair."

Lacey starts crying even harder.

"No! No! Of course not. We will go to salon. Right away."

"We will?" I ask.

"But of course!" Mom waves an arm wildly. "Is disaster!" And she springs into action. She orders Lacey to eat cookies and pours her a glass of milk. She scribbles a note for Dad and the boys: *Must fix emergency problem. Eat casserole in oven. Explain later.*

Then she finds a scarf, a bright red one, and she actually ties it on Lacey's head. Lacey's eyes are bugging out as Mom says, "Put scarf. No one will notice." When Mom whips out of the room to, "Put lipstick," I can't look at Lacey. I can't.

"Does she think," Lacey whispers, "that no one will notice the scarf?"

Carefully, I explain. "No, she talks like people do when they're online. You know, lots of short cuts. She means that no one will notice your hair because it's hidden by the scarf."

"But," says Lacey, "they *will* notice the scarf, right? I mean, I don't want to upset your mom, but the scarf is, like, bizarre."

"I know," I say. "I'm sorry."

Lacey starts to giggle. She waves an arm dramatically. "Is disaster!"

I sigh. "I know. Always."

Lacey's giggles stop as suddenly as they started. "She's funny, your mom. But nice. Really nice."

And then Mom's back in the room, hustling us out the door and into the car.

She's like a woman on a mission. She even speeds on the way to the salon as if this is an actual emergency. "We will go to Estelle. She will know what to do."

"Um," says Lacey, "who's Estelle?"

"She is wonderful hairdresser. You will see. She can fix."

I want to groan but I suppress it. Estelle is one of Mom's Bosnian buddies and she might be wonderful for Mom's idea of style, but for Lacey? I open my mouth to say we ought to go to the mall, but Lacey cuts me off. "Cool. I didn't really want to go to the mall."

Of course she doesn't want to go to the mall. Be seen wearing a red head scarf? Worse yet, be seen with Mom and me? I start wondering how I got into this. I mean, just a few short days ago, this whole scene could only have existed in my nightmares. I would have wakened and laughed at the strange imagination of the dreaming brain. Maybe this is a nightmare?

No, here we are at Estelle's place. Her salon is in the basement of her house. And there's Mom, already knocking at the door, and there's Estelle answering and they're jabbering in Bosnian, waving their arms. I sneak a peek at Lacey, and she looks scared. Not that I blame her. I'm nervous and I'm not even the one getting a haircut.

By the time Lacey is shampooed and sitting in the chair, I think she's on the verge of a major panic attack. Her eyes are darting around, her face is pink and the knuckles on her hands are white from the death grip she has on the purple cape she's wearing. Estelle and Mom are discussing the situation in Bosnian. Estelle is clicking a pair of scissors open and shut and brandishing a comb like a sword. Lacey looks like she's going to bolt when Estelle suddenly switches to English.

"How this happen to you?"

"Um, I got gum stuck in my hair."

"And you cut"—Estelle gestures wildly with the scissors—"like this?"

I wait for Lacey to tell how it was her psycho mom who cut like that, but she doesn't. She just nods her head.

"Okay," says Estelle. "I can fix. Make layers. But maybe we part hair on side instead of middle. Like so." Deftly, she parts Lacey's hair with her comb.

Lacey's eyes widen. Already, there's an improvement.

"And then...," says Estelle. And then she's snipping, combing, fluffing, completely absorbed in her task.

The rest of us stare into the mirror, watching the flash of those scissors, the slide of the comb. Nobody speaks. I glance at Mom and she's smiling. There's something else on her face too. Pride? Is she proud of Estelle? Of pretty Lacey? I can't tell, but I do know this. I'm suddenly jealous, fiercely jealous. There's Lacey, once again the center of attention. She even has *my* mom's attention! I was right. Really bad stuff doesn't happen to girls like Lacey. An image of her cold mother flashes into my mind, but I ignore it.

I ignore it again when Mom drops Lacey off at home. Lacey's hair looks fabulous, and she thanks Mom about ten times. But when she gets out of the car and turns toward her house, she takes a deep shaky breath. And another. Mom's busy watching for her chance to pull out in traffic, so only I see the look Lacey sends after us. It's the look of a puppy that's just been abandoned.

chapter nine

I spend the evening wondering if I should go back over to Lacey's and rescue her. What if Shiny Mom hits her? What if she takes the scissors to Lacey again? What if she didn't even let her in the house?

In the end, I do nothing. Not quite nothing. I look for quotes to describe Lacey, only that doesn't go anywhere either. I find one on a website for artists that might work, but I still don't feel like I know her well enough to be sure it's right.

Then I wonder what quote Lacey might give to me. If she sees what I want her to see, it'll be a quote about being independent. It'll describe someone who doesn't care what anyone else thinks. Someone who is their own person. She'll never find the real quote, if there even is one, about the girl who lives in dread. The girl who hasn't had a real friend for years because no one understands her dark fears and her nervous anger. The girl who doesn't know how to fix this.

The first thing I feel when I see Lacey at school is relief. She looks fine, no black eyes, no shaved head. In fact she looks great. The usual pack of girls has gathered around to admire her hair.

Lacey smoothes it carefully, bats her eyelashes and says, "Oh, I went to this great European place. Very exclusive." Then her boyfriend Chad shows up, and I swear I see drool forming at the side of his mouth.

"Chad," Lacey coos, "do you like the new me?"

"Cool," he says. And that's it. Now that I think about it, I don't believe I've ever heard Chad really talk. He does make sounds, and he does manage these one word sentences, but that's about it. He drapes an arm over Lacey and they stand there grinning. I glance around, half expecting a photographer to pop out of a locker and start taking pictures. I mean, they look like they're posing. Sick.

Lacey finally notices my existence in art class. She drops a note on my table that says, *I've got a surprise for you.*

I scribble, *I don't like surprises*, and drop my reply on her table.

She decides to be seen speaking to me in public. She sidles up to my table, looks the other way and whispers out the side of her mouth. "You don't like surprises?"

"No," I say.

"Oh, that's too bad. Should I just tell you then?"

I do an eye roll. "Sure, just tell me."

But before she can, the distinct sound of breaking glass crackles from the table behind us. Everyone cranes their head to see what happened, and there's Rav staring stonily at his broken mirror.

The guy beside him says, "Cool! Can I have it?"

Rav blinks. "Why?"

Mr. Ripley is there now too. "Yes, Eddy, why?"

Eddy grins. "Because it'll be perfect for my frame." He points at the work in progress on his table and says, "See?"

Sure enough, it's obvious that his frame has been made to look like a network of cracks. Sort of like a dried out mud puddle, cracks running every which way.

"Hmmm," says Mr. Ripley. "I see you're working on a theme."

"Yeah," someone says, "he's saying he's cracked."

"Either that or he's a crack head," someone sniggers.

"Well," says Mr. Ripley, "I'm reminded of a Leonard Cohen quote: *There's a crack in everything. That's how the light gets in.*"

Nice. Talk about putting a positive spin on things.

Lacey whispers, "I *love* that."

Matt, the guy across from me, breaks the spell. "There's a crack in my bum too. That's why the light shines outta my..."

"That'll do, Matt!" Mr. Ripley roars. "Everyone get back to work."

"Right," Lacey whispers to me. "So I'll bring the surprise to your place after school. I'll be there by three-thirty."

And she's gone, leaving me no chance to argue. So I go home after school and wait for her to show up.

She arrives carrying a big bag. "Here it is!" she bubbles. "Your surprise!"

I fold my arms across my chest. "What is it?"

"Let's go up to your room and I'll show you."

"Why do we have to go to my room?" I ask.

"Sable, relax. You'll like it, I promise. Come on!" And Lacey heads for the stairs. I can either stand there with my arms folded or follow her. I feel I have no choice but to follow; somehow this blond bimbo has started running my life. I'm going to have to find a way to put a stop to it.

I will reject her surprise.

But when I get to my room, the surprise is spilling out all over my bed. "See!" Lacey crows. "Makeup! I'm going to give you a makeover."

"No, you're not," I say.

"What? Oh, come on, don't be shy! You're going to love it, I promise."

"No, I won't," I say.

"But you will!" Lacey's lower lip goes into the pout. "Please, Sable. It's the least I can do after what your mom did for me." She puts her hands on her hips. "And besides, I have the most awesome plan for us."

"A plan? What plan?"

"It's like this. You sit down there on your chair, right?" She waits for me to do as she suggested, but I don't, so she sighs and goes on. "Then, while you're sitting there and I'm doing your makeup, we'll have this trust for each other, right? I mean, doing makeup is soooo personal, right? And then we can play Truth or Dare! Isn't that perfect?"

"No," I say, "that's retarded."

A bright pink spot of color appears in both of Lacey's cheeks. "Okay then, Ms. Party-pooper, what's your idea?"

Ms. Party-pooper? I can't think of a single response for that one. I'll have to let it pass. I refuse to stoop to her level. I lift my chin and very snottily ask, "Just exactly what do I need an idea for?"

She actually stamps her foot. "I cannot believe you are this dumb! We only have a few days left to hand in our quotes, and I bet you don't have a clue, do you?"

I stand there with my mouth opening and closing like a fish. I know I do this because after about the third time, I catch myself. She thinks *I'm* dumb? I sit in the chair. I only do this so that I can figure out how that's possible, but she takes it as a sign.

"Oh good! I'm so glad you've changed your mind." She grabs one of those wide stretchy hair bands, scrunches it over my head, pulls my hair through and carefully positions the band so that all my hair is skinned back from my face.

"You know," she says, "you have very pretty eyes. I can't wait to do them. But first"—and now she's coming at me with a tube—"we'll do the foundation."

chapter ten

By the time I recover the power of speech, Lacey is plucking my eyebrows. Okay, so maybe that's why I start talking again. I yell, "Ow! Stop it!"

She makes that little *tsk-tsk* sound and says, "No pain, no gain."

"That's for sports," I shout.

"Just chill, Sable," she soothes. "Who says it's for sports?"

"Everyone!"

"Well, I'm sure they won't mind us using

it too." Lacey keeps plucking. Then she says, "Oh-oh."

"What oh-oh?" I shriek. "What have you done?"

"Nothing. It's fine. I just noticed that you're starting to sweat a bit. We'll have to do the foundation over again."

"Of course I'm sweating! Do you have any idea how painful this is?"

"There you go," she says sweetly, "it *is* like sports. Pain, sweat, everything."

My options at this point are laughing or crying. I start laughing.

Lacey eyes me doubtfully. "You're not getting, like, hysterical, are you?"

I wipe my eyes. Shake my head. Take a deep breath. "No," I say, "I'm fine. But I think I need a break."

"A snack?" Lacey asks hopefully.

"Sure, why not. A snack." I stick my head out of the bedroom door, listen carefully, hear nothing and make a run for the kitchen. Lacey follows and is clearly disappointed when we don't find my mother.

"Where's your mom?"

I find a note from my mom on the counter and read it aloud, "Out having fun with boys."

"Jeez," says Lacey, "she doesn't seem like that type to me. Are you sure that's what it says?"

I grab a couple juice boxes and a container of cream cheese out of the fridge and hand Lacey a box of crackers from the cupboard. "I have two little brothers," I tell her.

"Oh," she says. She follows me back to my room in silence, but when we get there she adds, "You're so lucky."

"Believe me," I tell her, "you probably wouldn't think so if you had brothers."

"It's not just that," she says. "It's everything."

I can't think of anything to say because I want to say no, she's the lucky one, the popular, pretty one. She ought to get that, it's so obvious. And then I know what to say. "Truth or Dare?"

Lacey grabs a cracker and grins. "Okay. You first."

I've never played Truth or Dare, but I think I know how it works. "Truth. Why is this art project so important to you?"

"That's not how it's supposed to go, Sable. I'm supposed to get a choice between telling the truth or taking a dare. But I'll answer your question. I want to get a good grade because art is the only thing I like at school and I want to be an artist."

"Why do you want to be an artist?" I ask.

"Well, that's a stupid question. Why does anybody want to be anything? I just do. And besides, it's my turn now." She eyes me narrowly. "Truth or dare?" she asks.

"Truth," I say promptly.

"Hmmm," she says, "that tells me something already. Are you chicken?"

"Chicken of what?"

"I'm doing the asking. Are you afraid?"

How did she get to my worst question already? I try to stall for time. "Of what?" I repeat.

"Of dares!"

"No, of course not. I just thought that it

would be faster for us to get to know each other if we stick to the truth questions. Forget the dares."

"But that's not the rules," she says.

"Fine," I say, "but let's make another rule. We can hear the question and the dare before we decide which one we'll do."

"No way," she says. And this tells me something about her. Lacey likes to do things by the rules. Not a bad quality.

"Whatever," I say. "Now it's my turn. Truth or dare?"

"Dare," she answers promptly.

I don't have any idea about what I can dare her to do. "Um," I say. "Are you sure?"

"Yes," she says.

"Okay." Think, Sable. Come on. Think. Ah, I've got it. "I dare you to cut a chunk out of your mom's hair while she's sleeping."

Lacey turns pure white. "Oh my God!" she shrieks. "That's the stupidest dare I ever heard! You're supposed to dare me to make a prank phone call or something!"

"Well," I say, "that's the dare."

"Forget it. Tell you what. We'll go with your rule. We can hear the question and the dare, then decide."

I consider arguing the point but since I'm in control for once, I decide to be gracious. "Okay." Maybe I'm giddy with my success because I ask a useless question. "Have you ever kissed a boy?"

Lacey does an eye roll. "Well, duh, yes. Have you?"

"What's the dare?" I shoot back.

"I dare you to kiss a boy," she says.

"Okay, I choose truth. Yes, I have kissed a boy." She looks faintly surprised, and I don't tell her the only boys I've kissed are my brothers.

"My turn," I say. I'm starting to enjoy this game. "Let's see. Is your dad an artist?"

The frozen mom look appears on Lacey's face. "My dad?" she asks coldly. "What are you talking about?"

"You said your dad read that newspaper article about the mirrors, remember? When you told Mr. Ripley about your idea."

She goes perfectly still. "I did say that, didn't I?" she mutters.

"Yeah, you did."

"Oh well." She takes a deep breath and comes up with a huge fake smile. "Yes, he is an artist. A very good one."

"So that's why you want to be one too? So you can be like him and not your mom, right?" Lacey doesn't answer, so I babble on. "But the funny thing is, you sure look like your mom."

"Shut up," says Lacey.

"What?"

"I said, shut up. It's none of your business."

"But...," I begin.

"Look, maybe this wasn't a good idea. Most people, when they play Truth or Dare, they don't get so weird." Lacey eyes me angrily. "You're weird, you know that?"

A crappy thing happens. Tears start rolling down my face. I look away from her. Mutter softly, "Yeah, I know."

"Oh, man!" says Lacey.

"I'm sorry," I croak. "I can't help it. I got weirdness from my mother."

"Sure you did," she says softly. "Just like me."

I hiccup and ask, "What do you mean?"

"I mean," she says, "that I don't want to be like my mom but in some ways, I am. It's like I can't help it."

"You don't seem like her to me—except you're both pretty."

"Right," says Lacey. "Pretty. Sometimes I wish I wasn't. Boys think I'm just a body. Girls get jealous. Nobody thinks I have a brain."

"Oh," I say.

"Yeah, it sucks the way looks are such a big deal. Only...." Her voice trails away.

"Only what?" I ask.

Lacey wrinkles her nose, shakes her head. "I like it when things are beautiful. It makes me feel good. I like pretty clothes and shiny hair, sure, but other things too. Like beautiful music, or flowers, or sunsets, or poetry. I love that stuff."

"Yeah," I say, "it beats ugly."

"It really does."

"But what if the beautiful things don't mean anything? What if it's just superficial? What if the ugly stuff is stronger?" I ask.

"It isn't!" Lacy says vehemently. "Beauty is powerful."

"How do you know?"

Lacey tilts her head and studies me. "Truth or dare?" she asks.

I feel like maybe I've had an overdose of truth. I take a deep breath and say, "Dare."

chapter eleven

Lacey claps her hands. "Awesome! I dare you to let me give you a total makeover and then you'll see."

"See what?"

"The difference."

I have no idea what she thinks she can prove by giving me a makeover, but I shrug and say, "Okay. Go for it."

"Right." Lacey is all business now. "First you need to wash your face. Then I'll do your makeup. Then we're going shopping."

So that's what we do. I have to admit what she does with the makeup is surprising. Maybe I do have pretty eyes. At least with the eye shadow and mascara and my plucked eyebrows, they look bigger. And the blush brings out my cheekbones. And the lip-gloss shows off the fact that I have lips. It's only when we get to the mall and she insists that I try on a dark red T-shirt that things get tricky.

"I only wear black," I tell her.

"Why?" she asks.

"This is a dare, not the truth," I shoot back.

She plants her hands on her hips. "Then you have to finish the dare."

I guess she's got me there. Lacey hovers outside the change room while I put on the top. It fits snugly. Much more clingy than my usual black shirts. It's a shock to look in the mirror and see my body complete with breasts and a waist.

Lacey pokes her head around the curtain and crows, "I knew it! You're a babe!"

"Yeah, right," I scoff. But my eyes are glued to the mirror in the change room. It's as if a stranger is standing where my reflection ought to be.

"You have to buy it," Lacey orders. "Then walk around the mall with me."

Walk around in public like this? The very thought makes my blood run cold. Goosebumps spring up over every inch of my skin. Okay, not on my face. For some reason we don't get face goosebumps—thank God—but the rest of me is covered.

"What's wrong?" Lacey asks. "You look funny."

"I'm not wearing this in the mall!"

"Why not?"

"Because I'm not! It's not me. Get out of here so I can take this thing off."

"Jeez," says Lacey, "you're not scared, are you?"

"Of course not!"

"I think you are," she says. "Scared of wearing a T-shirt. Wow."

"I'm not scared," I insist. But my voice is weak.

"Listen, Sable. It's no big deal. If you don't want to wear it, fine." She narrows her eyes. "But I'm telling you, this is the perfect opportunity for you to find out what it's like to be me."

"What are you talking about?"

"Hmm," she says. "I can't really explain it in words. It's one of those things you have to *experience*."

"You think you're pretty smart, don't you?" I ask.

She tosses her hair. "Yes."

"Well, you're not," I retort. "There is no way that me wearing a T-shirt in a mall is going to change who I am. Or teach me anything."

"Oh really?" She says. "Prove it."

"This is stupid. I don't have to prove anything!"

"Fine, maybe not. But maybe *I* have something to prove, Sable. Did you ever think of that? Isn't it about time you thought about someone besides yourself for once?"

Oh. My. God. This girl thinks I'm self-centered? I put up a hand. "Okay. You win. I'll do it. And we'll see who's right."

Lacey grins, grabs my arm and hauls me out of the change room. She tells me to leave the top on and asks the clerk to cut off the tag when I go to pay for it. "That T-shirt looks really good on you," the clerk gushes.

"See?" Lacey says.

"Whatever," I say. I feel completely exposed. Naked. I want to hide behind a clothes rack. Lacey asks the clerk to give me a bag for my old shirt, and then she's tugging on my arm again, leading me out of the store. Into the wide-open mall.

"Now," Lacey instructs, "pay close attention. There's a group of guys up there. We're going to walk past them, and I want you to look at them."

"What?" I blurt. With an effort, I force my mind to focus on this new threat. "Why?"

"So you can see them looking at you."

I fold my arms across my chest. "No," I mumble, "we don't want to be seen."

"Huh?" says Lacey.

"I mean, they're not going to look at me."

There is no way I'm looking at the boys. The only place I ever look when walking in a mall is at the ground or off into the distance. I never look at people and as far as I know, they never look at me.

"They are *so* going to look at you, and if you don't notice, you'll just tell me I was wrong, and I'm not!" Lacey's blue eyes are sparking with determination.

"What was the point of this again?" I ask.

"We're proving that beauty has power. Now be quiet. Here they come. Just put a tiny smile on your face. Here we go!"

She is so into this, honest to God, you'd think we were about to embark on a mission to save the planet. I try to do what she says. I paste a smile on my face and start walking beside Lacey.

"Look up!" Lacey hisses. "And forget the smile. Too fake."

My smile is fake? Well, of course it is. I glance up to see what her smile looks like and suddenly, there are the boys, right in front of us. And they are looking at us. In fact they are staring, but I don't make eye contact with them. They're fixated on places well below eye level. It's only in the last millisecond before our pass is complete—too right, this is like sports—that one of the guys flicks his gaze upward. And he raises an eyebrow as if to ask...what?

Lacey waits about two seconds, and then she starts doing a wiggle, sort of like football players do after they score a touchdown. "See!" she gloats. "I told you."

"Okay," I say, "you were right. They looked. But it was creepy, and I didn't like it, and it didn't make me feel powerful."

"Huh?" says Lacey.

"It made me feel like...a thing."

"Really?" Lacey's brows furrow as she thinks about this. "But see, if you wanted, you could get them to pay attention to you. Maybe ask you out on a date. Isn't that power? Getting what you want?"

"That's sick," I say.

She blinks at me. "Sick?"

"Yeah, I think that's more like *them* getting what they want."

"You're really shy, aren't you?" Lacey asks.

"What?" I sputter.

"Well..." She shrugs. "You are. And you pretend you aren't with this whole tough girl act."

My head is spinning. How is it possible that this girl sees through me? And how did she figure me out just by seeing that I don't think it's great to have guys checking me out like I'm a choice on the dessert menu?

"I'm not like you," I tell her.

"Jeez, Sable, I didn't say that. You're so serious all the time. Lighten up, why don't you? Have some fun."

"You know," I say, "I have to go now."

"Fine," she sighs. "Maybe I'll come by to pick up my stuff tomorrow?"

"Sure, whatever," I answer.

And we go our separate ways.

chapter twelve

It figures that the second I walk through our door Mom is there. Of course she starts making a really big deal out of the "new me." "Sable! Look at you!" Something, something in Bosnian, arms spread wide with delight. "This is amazing!"

"Don't get used to it," I tell her.

Dad wanders in, stops dead and says, "Well, don't you look nice."

The boys, scenting prey, tumble into the room and start sniggering. "Gross, Sable! You look like a girl."

I ignore them and tell Mom, "I'm not really hungry. I think I'll just go up to my room."

"Sable, you should eat dinner! You are not thinking to be dieting, are you?"

An eye roll is totally called for. "You read too many magazines, Mom." I bolt for my room with every intention of peeling off the makeup and red top, but when I get there, I don't. Instead I look at myself in the mirror. For a long time.

The girl in the mirror is not ugly. She might even be sort of, almost, pretty.

I remember Mr. Ripley telling us in art class that colors merge into each other. We had to paint a portrait, and things weren't going well for most of us. I mean, if we were painting monsters or something, the pictures would have been great. Mr. Ripley tried to help us out, and one of the things he did was demonstrate how color is reflected in human skin. He got several different colored pieces of fabric and held them under his face. It was sort of cool, because when he held up bright blue, his skin changed color. Not a lot, but we could see a difference. When he changed to orange, his skin was tinged with warmth. When he used olive green, he looked sick.

"This shade of green doesn't agree with my skin tone," he said. "Which is too bad because for a while, when I was a kid, the coolest stuff to wear was army gear."

We all laughed and we got the point. I'm getting it again now with the red top. This color makes me look...brighter. Even cheerful. But, big deal. It's just skin deep isn't it? It doesn't change who I am. And the whole experience in the mall, with people seeing me as someone else—that was freaky. Okay, so maybe a tiny part of me liked being admired by the boys. Only what good does that do? What will it change? There's no way it'll change the world. I mean, there's nothing wrong with liking beauty. I like it too, but it's not as if....

Wait a minute! There's the strand of an idea here. The idea is so fragile and strange that I can't quite catch hold of it. It feels like it could disappear the way dreams do in that moment of waking. I told Lacey that beauty isn't powerful. But what if it is? What if beauty *can* change the world?

I start pacing. Back and forth, back and forth. Maybe I need a definition of beauty? A really big definition. I'll bet Mr. Ripley has one. He has lots of definitions for art.

I keep pacing. There's a knock at my door. My mother's voice. "What are you doing in there, Sable? Exercising?"

Overkill Mom strikes again. I throw open my door and say, "Mom, what's beautiful?"

She stands there reorganizing her thoughts, her mouth opening and closing like a fish, and I think, Oh great, I got that from her too. Finally she says, "Life. Love." She gestures grandly. "Everything!"

"Everything?" I ask. "What about bombs? Aliens? Pollution?"

"Okay," she says. "Not everything."

"Thanks," I say. And close the door.

She knocks.

"I'm not exercising!" I yell. "I'm figuring something out! Please, Mom, just leave me alone for a while!"

"You are beautiful," she yells back.

I open the door. "Even if that were true, does it *really* matter?"

She shrugs. "It depends. Why you are asking this?"

"I don't know yet," I tell her. "I'll let you know when I know."

"Okay," she says. And *she* closes the door. The woman is learning.

Five minutes later, I have my black shirt on over the red top and as I pass through the kitchen I tell Mom, "I'm going to take Lacey's stuff over to her house."

She looks like she wants to argue, but all she ends up saying is, "Fine. But if you are there after dark, call for ride."

I'm not really going to Lacey's to return her makeup, even though I do have it with me. I'm going to ask her some questions. Very likely, she won't be there. A warm June evening, a Friday at that, she has a boyfriend...chances are I won't see her. But this sudden need to understand something I feel so close to understanding—it makes me go anyway.

chapter thirteen

I'm at Lacey's house in no time. It must have taken fifteen minutes, but it seems like I blinked and I'm there. Now what? I look at the house, that ugly house, and I don't get it. Why is it so neglected on the outside but so crazy perfect inside? It makes no sense. It doesn't match the people who live there because Lacey and her mean mom look great on the outside, perfect clothes, hair, all that. Maybe her mom leaves it like this to annoy the neighbors? Maybe she figures it's a man's job and her husband is so busy doing art he never bothers?

I'm not going to figure it out by standing here. I march around the back and knock on the door. Nothing happens. I knock again. Still nothing. Well, that's what I expected. But then, I hear a small sound. "*Psst*!"

I look around but don't see anyone. Then I hear it again. It's coming from the far side of the house. I pick my way through the weeds and crane my head around the corner. And there's Lacey, peeking out a window.

"Sable," she whispers, "come here."

"What are you doing?" I ask.

"Keep your voice down!" she hisses. "I don't want my mom to hear you."

I glance around nervously but don't see Psycho Mom. "Don't you think she heard the knocking?" I whisper.

Lacey grimaces. "For sure. But she never answers the door unless she's expecting someone."

"Oh," I say. "Well, I brought your stuff. But I guess I should go, hey?"

"No, just wait. She's going out in a minute. Then I'll let you in."

Sure enough, I hear the clatter of heels and a door opening. I flatten myself against the wall and hold my breath.

"Lacey?" Psycho Mom's voice comes clearly through the window. "I'm going now. I'll lock the doors."

"Okay," Lacey answers.

"Love you," the voice calls. Did I hear that right? Then the heels clatter again, the sound fades. A door on the far side of the house opens and closes. A car engine starts. She's gone.

"Sable?" Lacey's face appears at the window again. "You can come in now."

She lets me in through the back door, and the inside of the house is even whiter than I remember. I can't help it, I have to ask, "Lacey, why is your place so strange?"

"What do you mean?" she asks. She's stalling, I can tell.

"You know. So perfect inside and so messy outside. Do you guys have allergies or something?"

She shrugs. "Or something."

"So what's the something?" I ask.

"Someone's sure nosey today."

"Sorry," I mutter.

"But you know what?" Lacey doesn't wait for me to answer. "Maybe we could finish our game of Truth or Dare."

"I thought we *were* finished," I say.

"Why did you come here then? I know you didn't just want to return my stuff."

I sigh. I tell her the plain truth. "I came because I'm confused. And I need to talk about it."

Lacey's eyes widen. "Wow. I think that's the first time I ever got a straight answer out of you, Sable."

"Thanks," I say. "I think."

Lacey giggles. "Come on, I want to show you something." She leads the way into the living room. Or rather, the room most people would use as a living room. I'm thinking, Oh good, I get to see it. But some things are best left unseen.

It's like a carnival freak show. Standing shoulder to shoulder, lining every wall, are giant Barbie dolls. No, not Barbies. They're mannequins, and their solid blank faces stare across the open floor at each other, past each other, past us.

"What," I breathe, "is this?"

"This is a studio," Lacey says.

"Oh! Right! So your dad makes...fake people?"

She shakes her head. "Not my dad. My mom."

"Your mom?" I repeat. "She's an artist too?"

"If you can call it that. She's a fashion designer. Or more like a wannabe. Anyway, she keeps bringing these mannequins home, and she's supposed to be making clothes for them. Only...she never buys any fabric."

"They're creepy," I blurt.

"Yeah," says Lacey, "I know." She stands there with her arms folded, staring at them as if she could stare them down.

"Um," I say, "can we get out of here?"

"What? Oh. Sure."

I bolt for the kitchen but I don't feel any better. Those dummies are still too close.

Maybe Lacey sees how edgy I am because she says, "Let's go to my room instead."

And her room is normal. Pictures on the wall, clothes on the floor, a flowery bed, a desk strewn with a mix of paper, perfume and jewellery.

"Whew," I say.

"I know," she says.

We both sink down at the same moment, her onto the bed, me into a pile of fluffy pillows. About a million questions are zipping around in my head, tripping over each other, fighting to be the first past my lips.

"Okay," says Lacey, "I can tell you're dying to ask me some stuff. So I'm just going to tell you and get it over with. My mom is nuts. My dad is long gone. And that's it."

I take this in. Slowly. More questions start bubbling in my boggled brain, but once again, Lacey cuts to the chase.

"I lied about having a dad because I wish I had one. Mine left about five years ago when my mom started losing it. My mom is mostly harmless. She holds a steady job, keeps up with the bills. That thing with the scissors, she's not usually that bad. It's just her disorder—she's obsessive-compulsive. She can't *stand* anything icky. I mean, that's why the outside is so grungy, right? It's too much for her to control, so she ignores it."

"But...," I search for the right way to ask, "are you okay with that?"

"I have to be," she says fiercely. "She's my mom, right? So don't go telling anyone about this, Sable, like I'm some sort of case. There's no way I'm leaving her. We're fine."

She's watching me steadily and there's no lie in her blue eyes. But there's something else lurking in her gaze, something familiar. Fear. "I won't tell," I whisper.

She sighs. "Thanks." She pauses, and then she adds softly, "It feels good to tell someone about it, you know?"

An unfamiliar rush of warmth washes over me. She's saying she trusts me! Me. "Yeah," I say, "I guess it does."

Lacey grins. "Funny how that works, huh?"

I nod.

She's watching me, waiting, as if she's expecting something. And I know what it is. It's my turn to share a deep dark secret. I don't have any, except for the doom thing. Now I need to stall for time. There are some interesting pictures in her room, stuff with vibrant colors and swooping lines. "Nice art," I say.

"Thanks," says Lacey.

I look more closely and notice a loopy *L* signature on most of them. "You did these?" I ask. And I don't manage to disguise the surprise in my voice.

"Yeah," she says.

"Wow! They're really good." They are.

"You think?" Lacey scrutinizes the portrait nearest her and shrugs. "They're okay. I'm working on it." She returns her expectant gaze to me.

I sigh and tell her. "I feel that doom is near."

"Huh?" says Lacey.

"Doom," I say shakily.

"You mean you're, like, afraid of something?" she asks.

"Yeah," I say. "That's it. I'm afraid of everything."

"Whoa," she says. "You can't be afraid of everything!"

"Why not?" I ask.

"Because," she says, "that would be too much." She leans forward. "Are you afraid of flowers?"

"No."

"Butterflies?"

"No."

"Puppies?"

"No!" I shout. "That's not what I mean!"

Lacey leans back and asks, "So, what do you mean?"

"I mean I'm afraid the world will end. I'm afraid of aliens, the flu, holes in the ozone. I'm even afraid of other people most of the time!"

"Hah," says Lacey. "Too funny."

"No!" I say hotly, "Not funny!"

"You're actually afraid of aliens?" she asks.

"Aren't you?" I counter.

"Um, no. I mean I might be, if they were real." She waves a hand. "I don't have time to worry about stuff like that. What you need, Sable, is a real problem."

"I need a real problem?" I can't believe she said that. Isn't doom a problem?

"Yes." Lacey nods. "You do." She ponders for a moment then brightens dramatically. "I've got it! You should get a boyfriend. They cause all sorts of problems. I mean, look at Chad. We were supposed to go out to a movie tonight, right? Only he suddenly needs to do an emergency workout at the gym with his buds. He's such a loser."

Right. I felt sorry for her for about three minutes because of her nutty mom and all, but no more. She's ridiculous. "I do not need a boyfriend problem. Thanks anyway."

"Oh yeah," she says. "You're afraid of people too. Hmmm. But then, this could be perfect. You overcome your fear of people by getting a boyfriend, and abracadabra! Everything's great."

"You know what?" I don't wait for her to answer. "I just remembered what I wanted to talk to you about. And it isn't boyfriends. It's about changing the world."

chapter fourteen

When Lacey gets over her fit of giggles, she says, "Um, Sable, changing the world is, like, impossible."

"No," I say, "it can't be. 'Cause if it is, then I'm toast."

In a gentle voice, Lacey asks, "Have you always been so messed up?"

I shrug. "I guess. It's no big deal. I'm used to it."

"Hmm," she says. "Okay. I guess I'm used to it too. My mom, right? So what's your deal?"

"Well, I don't have a mental disorder, if that's what you think. What I have is this feeling that I have to *do* something. Because if I don't then all the crap in the world probably *will* give me a disorder."

I get to my feet and start pacing. "For a long time, I've been trying to figure it out. I think about the problems, but I never find any answers. Only today you said something that gave me a new idea."

Lacey's eyes go round. "I did?"

"Yeah. You said beauty is power. And that's the exact opposite of what I've been thinking. I've been thinking about how powerful all the horrible stuff is and about ways I can fight it. But maybe I've had it all backward."

Lacey jumps to her feet too. "I get it! So you...you." She slumps down again. "Okay, I don't get it."

I throw my hands up in frustration. "Neither do I! But I know there's something to this. We have to think big. As in, beauty is way more than just being pretty."

"What's wrong with being pretty?" Lacey asks.

"Nothing. But don't you think just using beauty to get attention is sort of shallow?" I rush on before she can get offended. "I mean, what if the beauty was deep? What if it was everywhere?"

"Like art," Lacey says. "I love art. All kinds."

"Yes! All kinds of art, music, original thoughts, everything. And if people had that sort of beauty all around, if they spent time with it, then..."

"Then they'd be happy!" Lacey says.

"Well, *maybe*," I say.

"Art makes me happy. It's how I figure stuff out. Don't you think creating beautiful things would make everyone happy?" she asks.

"I think it would help. But there'd still be problems," I say glumly. "It's not like the flu will notice that everything's gorgeous. And aliens could have entirely different taste."

"Jeez," she says, "now you're getting, like, negative again. Why are you so scared?"

I know the answer. I do. But if I say it out loud, it'll sound so lame.

I take a deep breath and say it anyway. "I've been like this since I was three, when my dad was shot and my mom was so scared.... That's all the world was, for days and days, just this huge ball of suffocating terror. And I guess it just never went away."

"God," Lacey whispers. "That's so awful. You remember all that?"

"Not really. Not the details. I just know what happened. And I remember the feeling."

"And you can't forget that stuff? Just make yourself think about nice things?"

I stare at her. A fight breaks out in my head. Is it really that simple? Just change how I think? Impossible. I can't pretend problems don't exist.

"Is that what you do?" I ask. "Just forget about your problems and they go away?"

"No! I'm not a total slacker. Okay, maybe I am, sometimes. But why should I beat myself up trying to fix things I can't fix? That's just, like, useless."

She's right. That is useless. But like the light shining through a crack, I see my answer. There is no point in trying to fight ugly with more ugly. No point in responding to fear by trying to be scarier or nastier. Why react like that? Why not be free and choose how to act, instead of being controlled by outside forces? Why not hold hands with all that's beautiful?

"Lacey," I say, "you're a genius."

"I am?"

"Yeah. You are."

"Good," she says, "but do you mind telling me why?"

"Because of the way you see the world. I've been so focused on the scary stuff and feeling so hopeless...so weak." I take a deep breath and when I exhale, I feel lighter. "Just thinking about creating beauty—that makes me feel stronger. Like I can do something big. You showed me how I can change my appearance with just a little makeup and different clothes. If it's that easy to change me..."

Lacey grins. "It wasn't *that* easy!"

I laugh. "Okay, maybe not. But it wasn't so hard either. What I'm trying to say is that beauty could be my key to courage. My way to change the world. My way to conquer doom."

chapter fifteen

For the last art class of grade nine, Mr. Ripley displays our mirrors on the wall around the room. "Excellent work, people," he says. He points out a frame trimmed with papier-mâché roses. "We've got something romantic here." He shifts to the next one, a metallic frame studded with rivets. "And something industrial here. We've got it all."

He moves on, commenting on each mirror. When he gets to mine, I'm not embarrassed. I didn't do the snake after all. Instead, I went for a vine effect, tendrils of growth winding round the mirror. The best part is the quote on the back, the one Lacey gave me by Ralph Waldo Emerson: *"Though we travel the world over to find the beautiful, we must carry it with us or we find it not."*

The last mirror is Lacey's. She too changed her design. Her frame is the yin-yang symbol, black circling to meet white, with the dots painted onto the surface of the glass. Behind her mirror is the quote I found by Vincent Van Gogh: *"I tell you, the more I think, the more I feel that there is nothing more truly artistic than to love people."*

"Beautiful work," Mr. Ripley states. "Very classic design. Lacey, I think we all owe you a big thank-you for suggesting this project. I'm certain everyone learned something about art on this one."

Lacey smiles, tosses her hair, says, "For sure, Mr. Ripley."

Then she looks at me and I'm able to ignore the pink bow on her head. I mean, that's who she is, right? She tried to convince me to wear a blue one to match my new blue top. There was no way.

But I convinced her to do something. We're going to spend the summer fixing up the outside of her house. She loved the idea. "The power of beauty everywhere! You *are* going to change the world, Sable."

I don't know about the world, but I figured her house was a good place to start. I got stuck with the dirt and the weeds because Lacey made up this huge story about the possibility of discovering new life forms. She said I might find a plant that cures cancer. I told her that was retarded; she told me to stop being negative. She has a point. I think the main reason I got the yard was because she doesn't trust my artistic skills for painting the house. Her mom agreed to let her paint it however she wants, and Lacey is planning a huge mural with a mirror right in the middle of it.

"The mirror will reflect your garden, Sable. Won't that be cool?"

It will be. Very cool.

Other titles in the Orca Currents series